Stop Loving the World

SERIES EDITORS
Joel R. Beeke & Jay T. Collier

Interest in the Puritans continues to grow, but many people find the reading of these giants of the faith a bit unnerving. This series seeks to overcome that barrier by presenting Puritan books that are convenient in size and unintimidating in length. Each book is carefully edited with modern readers in mind, smoothing out difficult language of a bygone era while retaining the meaning of the original authors. Books for the series are thoughtfully selected to provide some of the best counsel on important subjects that people continue to wrestle with today.

Stop Loving the World

William Greenhill

Edited by
Jay T. Collier

Reformation Heritage Books
Grand Rapids, Michigan

Stop Loving the World
© 2011 by Reformation Heritage Books

Published by
Reformation Heritage Books
2965 Leonard St., NE
Grand Rapids, MI 49525
616-977-0889 / Fax: 616-285-3246
e-mail: orders@heritagebooks.org
website: www.heritagebooks.org

Originally titled "Being against the Love of the World" and published as an appended sermon to *The Sound Hearted Christian* (London, 1670).

Printed in the United States of America
11 12 13 14 15 16/10 9 8 7 6 5 4 3 2

Library of Congress Cataloging-in-Publication Data

Greenhill, William, 1591-1671.
  [Being against the love of the world]
  Stop loving the world / William Greenhill ; edited by Jay T. Collier.
      p. cm. — (Puritan treasures for today)
  "Originally titled 'Being against the love of the world' and published as an appended sermon to The sound hearted Christian (London, 1670)"—T.p. verso.
  Includes bibliographical references and index.
  ISBN 978-1-60178-118-5 (pbk. : alk. paper) 1. Church and the world—Sermons. 2. Sermons, English—17th century. 3. Puritans—Sermons. I. Collier, Jay T., 1974- II. Title.
  BR115.W6G72 2011
  261—dc22
                                        2010049368

For additional Reformed literature, both new and used, request a free book list from Reformation Heritage Books at the above address.

Table of Contents

Preface

I imagine a title like *Stop Loving the World* evokes a strong response. While some people are willing to admit it more than others, most of us feel some tinge of resistance to being told not to love the world. Maybe your reaction is defensive. (*Who said I love the world? How dare you judge me like that?*) But more likely, the resistance comes in the form of a challenge. (*What do you mean that we should stop loving the world? John 3:16 says that God loves the world, so why not us too? Come on, why all the Puritan prudishness?*) The truth of the matter is that the mandate to stop loving the world is straight from the Bible: "Love not the world, neither the things that are in the world" (1 John 2:15). So whether we react defensively or offensively, we must begin by wrestling with the fact that it is God who tells us to stop loving the world.

Could it be that the reason for such reactions is that we do love the world too much? It is true that some people present an imbalanced view that sees little to no value in the world around them. And surely we must seek a responsible understanding of what the biblical injunction to stop loving the world really means. But in spite of such abuses and taking proper interpretation into account, sensitive Christians will readily admit that one of our greatest temptations is to make more of the world than we do of its Creator. Without realizing it, we cling to the things of this world with ardent affection. Even good, wholesome, God-given gifts are cherished more than the Giver.

Wealth, fame, and power are among the most desirable things that this world offers. We adore stuff, be it money, land, or other material conveniences and comforts. We cherish the good opinion of others, desiring honor among men. And we love to be in control, influencing the way things happen in this world and having our will be done. Each of these things has its proper place, yet we so easily expect them to be our source of joy.

The problem of loving the world is intensified in our day by the glamour of technological advances and the accessibility of so many things. The Internet virtually puts the world at our fingertips. You can sell or acquire just about anything at the click of a button, generate a multitude of "friends" and "fans" on blogs and social networking sites, and mobilize the masses with online campaigns. In this novel realm of virtual reality, the charms of the world appear ever at hand.

While our highly technological society, steeped in rampant materialism, is certainly prone to loving the world, the problem with worldliness and our resistance to being told to oppose it is nothing new. Love for the world has been a problem for mankind since the Fall, when Adam and Eve cherished a piece of fruit more than the will of the One who created the fruit. It is an age-old problem that will persist until Christ returns, which is why the Holy Spirit inspired the apostle John to tell us to stop loving the world. Since this is a problem that the people of God have always had to battle against, we should avail ourselves of the counsel of Christians throughout the ages in our pursuit of a remedy for loving the world.

A good place to start is with the Puritans. Their sermons and books were often concerned with this topic, providing excellent resources for suppressing undue love for the world. To this end, I commend this book by William Greenhill (1598–1671). It was originally titled "Being against the Love of the World" and published as an appended sermon to his book, *The Sound Hearted Christian* (London, 1670). The text of this sermon is rather lengthy — much longer than the other appended sermons — and was likely preached in more than one service or expanded from the original delivery for publication purposes. Believing that the sermon stands well enough on its own as a book, we have updated the language for modern readers, divided it into convenient chapters, and added subheadings in order to help this piece of wise counsel speak to a new generation. It states rather concisely the Puritan concern and solution to the ever-common problem of loving the world.

Before you read this book, it might help you to realize that Greenhill felt the lure of the world and the pain associated with denying it his love. Long before he preached on the topic, he was challenged to put his principles into practice. Multiple times in his life, Greenhill was removed from respectable and influential places of employment due to his convictions. One of these times was in 1636. Greenhill had become a minister in Oakley, Suffolk, and he also participated in two prominent preaching posts in Suffolk and Norwich. These places of honor provided him a comfortable living and an opportunity to make a difference for Christ. But in 1633, King Charles I, who sorely opposed the Puritans, reissued *The Book of Sports* and declared that ministers who refused to read it from their pulpits would lose their positions. Like many Puritans, Greenhill refused to read it to his people and was removed from office.

What the Puritans found so offensive was that the book encouraged worldly entertainment on the Lord's Day. In effect this was a dual trial for Greenhill and others on how much they loved the world. First, following *The Book of Sports* would mean relinquishing part of the Lord's Day — a whole day set aside for a more direct and explicit expression of our love for the Lord — in order to display one's love for the world. Second, ministers were tempted to read this royal declaration under the threat of losing their employment. It was not that Greenhill believed that recreation and places of honor were illegitimate. Rather, he was convinced that giving way to these temptations would betray a greater love for the things of this world than love for the God that gave them to him.

Greenhill's loss occurred long before he published this sermon, and he never refers to these personal struggles in the course of his message. Nevertheless, it serves to illustrate that Greenhill experienced the same sort of struggles he encouraged others to stand against. When tested, he was willing to give up good, godly positions in order to maintain a greater love for God. Greenhill stood in the trenches with his fellow brothers and sisters, giving counsel that had obviously been tested and tried in his own life.

One other thing should be noted about the Puritan call to stop loving the world. The Puritans have been portrayed as prudish stuffed shirts who wanted to withdraw altogether from the world. To cut through the caricature, we should note that Greenhill presents a balanced understanding of what it means to love the world. In the midst of this soul-searching message on loving the world, he is careful not to burden us with unreasonable expectations. Don't get me wrong; this is a very convicting book. But Greenhill avoids the mentality that denies the goodness of creation by distinguishing between properly *using* the world and *loving* it. He calls us to work with the things we have been given as an expression of our love for the Giver. Recognizing this, we see that the call to stop loving the world is not ultimately about what we should not do; it is a means to the positive goal of delighting in God. Our problem, however, is that we are entangled in a love affair with the things God has created. The world promises to satisfy us with itself, and we run to it instead of God. The world sells us a bill of goods that it can never fulfill, and we accept it.

Perhaps the reason people react so strongly against the Puritans is because we do in fact love the world. If you are anything like me, you need to hear the challenging, yet encouraging, message of this book. In it, Greenhill provides us with a healthy antidote to our love affair with the world. He explains what it means to love the world, exposes the dangers of cherishing it, shares how we ought to relate to it, and gives encouraging directions for removing our hearts from it. It is a book with a timeless message, demonstrating the relevance of the Puritans for today. I pray it spurs you on to live in such a way that shows that the world and all its charms are not what you live for. Rather, may you live in the world and use it in such a way that people clearly see that your heart belongs to the Christ and Creator of this world.

Jay T. Collier
Grand Rapids, Michigan
November 2010

CHAPTER 1

Concerning the World and Our Love for It

Love not the world, neither the things that are in the world.

— 1 John 2:15

John was the beloved disciple of Christ, and he wrote this epistle to those who were dear to Christ. His great aim was to confirm them in the faith of Christ and to encourage them in holiness and love, as may appear in 1 John 3:23: "This is his commandment, That we should believe on the name of his Son Jesus Christ, and love one another, as he gave us commandment." In the second chapter, verses 1–2, he lays down a remedy against the infirmities of weak Christians, that if any sinned, they had an advocate with the Father, Jesus Christ the Righteous. And lest that should be abused and men take liberty to sin (seeing there was such a remedy), he confronts them with keeping the commandments of the Lord in verses 3–6. This was a reminder that if they have any benefit by Christ, they will love Christ, and if they love Christ, they will keep the commands of Christ and walk as Christ walked. In verses 7–11, he instructs them in love, showing that it is both a new and an old commandment, in diverse respects. And then he speaks particularly to "little children" in verse 12, to "young men" in verse 13, and to "fathers" in verse 14. He tells them in the text that they must not love the world and the things that are in it. To do so is a great impediment both to holiness of life and love one to another. The words of this text will afford us two observations.

First, even saints are prone to love the world. There would not be a prohibition against loving the world unless we were naturally inclined to it. Yes, Christians are too apt to love the world and the things of the world. There is a great suitableness between the world and our corrupt hearts and natures. Pleasures, profits, honors, and things of this nature suit our fancies, our affections, our dispositions, and our inclinations. Therefore the apostle says, "Love not the world."

The second observation is that those who are in a state of grace — whether they are little children, young men, or fathers — should not love the world. "Love not the world, neither the things that are in the world."

Having made these observations, I will endeavor to address these things:

- What is meant by "the world," and what it is to love it

- Some reasons why we should not love the world (chapter 2)

- Some questions about how we relate to God's creation (chapter 3)

- Some applications of the doctrine (chapter 4)

- Further motives for not loving the world (chapter 5)

- Directions for getting our hearts off the world (chapter 6)

What "the World" Means

There are three main ways to understand the word "world":

1. "World" refers to the visible heavens and earth, with all the creatures in them, as they came from the hand of God. Genesis 1:1 tells us, "In the beginning God created the heaven and the earth." And after that, we are told of particular things that were created. In the New Testament, we are told that "all things were made by him," and that "he was in the world, and the world was made by him" (John 1:3, 10). The world, and all things in it, were made by Christ. God employed Christ in making the world and the things of the world. As a result, all things on earth are the workmanship of God and Christ, and are understood by the word "world."

2. "World" means the customs, manners, worship, and fashions of the world. Romans 12:2 says: "Be not conformed to this world, but be ye transformed." That is, do not be conformed to the customs and manners of the world, to its worship and fashions. We also see this in Colossians 2:20–22: "Wherefore if ye be dead with Christ from the rudiments of the world, why, as though living in the world, are ye subject to ordinances…after the commandments and doctrines of men?" Here, "world" is to be understood as the rudiments of men, the ways of men, the worship of men, and the ways of men in the worship of God. So you can see that "world" implies the customs, fashions, manners, and worship of the world. Elsewhere, these are called "weak and beggarly elements" (Gal. 4:9) and "the tradition of men" (Col. 2:8).

3. "World" means the pomp and splendor of the world, which Satan makes use of to further his kingdom and interest as well as to hinder the kingdom and interest of Christ. It is the abuse of the glory and greatness of God's creation, the excellencies and gifts of men, and the profits and pleasures of the world. So in Galatians 6:14 Paul says, "God forbid that I should glory, save in the cross of our Lord Jesus Christ, by whom the world is crucified unto me, and I unto the world." That is, "I am crucified to the pomp, glory, and splendor of the world, and all that is good according to the world. And the world is crucified unto me. It is a dead thing to me, and I am a dead thing to it." Paul elsewhere tells how Demas

"loved this present world" (2 Tim. 4:10), abandoning the ministry for the things, the pleasures, the profits, the honors, the comforts, and the contents of the world.

So then, "love not the world." Do not love the creatures of the world, the customs and fashions of the world, or the splendor, pomp, glory, and worship of the world. These three meanings of "world" are all understood here in our text.

What It Is to Love the World

1. To love the world is to highly esteem it, holding it in a high account. Christ said that the things that are of high account with men are an abomination to God. When we hold the world and the things of it in high esteem, we love the world. Those in Luke 14, when they were invited to the great feast, held their farms, their oxen, their wives, and the things of the world in higher account than the things of Christ. When these things are highly esteemed, we are said to love the world.

Many men would think that they had it made if they had the world. They say, "I would be happy if I had such an estate, such honors, such greatness." Consider Psalm 144:12–15:

> That our sons may be as plants grown up in their youth; that our daughters may be as corner stones, polished after the similitude of a palace: that our garners may be full, affording all manner of store: that our sheep may bring forth thou-

sands and ten thousands in our streets: that our
oxen may be strong to labour; that there be no
breaking in, nor going out; that there be no com-
plaining in our streets. Happy is that people, that
is in such a case.

Here David speaks on behalf of the men of the
world; they are happy men who are all prosperous and
successful. But he corrects them thus: "Happy is that
people, whose God is the LORD." Jonah highly esteemed
his gourd that perished in a night. The Jews highly
esteemed their temple. So we are said to love the world
when we set too high a value and estimation on the
things of the world.

2. We love the world when our thoughts are fixed on the
world. What a person loves, their thoughts are much
upon. "O how love I thy law," said David. "It is my meditation all the day" (Ps. 119:97). We meditate most on the
things we love. Now when our thoughts are consumed
by the world, when it is in our thoughts early and late,
we love the world and the things of it. Men are full of
thoughts for the world — the pleasures, the honors, the
profits, the contents, the delights of the world. Their
thoughts are taken up with these things. James 4:13 says,
"Go to now, ye that say, To day or to morrow we will
go into such a city, and continue there a year, and buy
and sell, and get gain." Their thoughts were fixed on the
world, buying and selling, and getting gain. By this they
testified of their love for the world. So in Psalm 49:11,

"Their inward thought is, that their houses shall continue for ever, and their dwelling places to all generations; they call their lands after their own names." All their thoughts were taken up and busied with these things, which demonstrated their love for the world. Likewise, Philippians 3:19 speaks of earthly minded men. When men's minds are on the earth and the things of the world, they love the earth and they love the world. They are inhabitants of the earth, seeking an inheritance here. So that is the second thing in which the love of the world consists: to have our thoughts taken up with the world, to mind the world, and to be carried toward the world.

3. Men are said to love the world when they desire the world. What men and women love, they desire much. Their desires are strong that way and run after those things. Love is a desire to be united with the thing loved. You know what is said in the commandments, "Thou shalt not covet thy neighbour's house, thou shalt not covet thy neighbour's wife, nor his manservant, nor his maidservant, nor his ox, nor his ass, nor any thing that is thy neighbour's" (Ex. 20:17). When there is a covetous desire in the soul, that shows the soul is in love with the thing. Oh, how the desires of men are carried after and so strongly affectionate for the things of the world!

4. Love for the world is found in setting the heart on the things of the world. Psalm 62:10 warns us: "If riches increase, set not your heart upon them." Many people

set their hearts on the things of the world. As we see in
Hosea 4:17, "Ephraim is joined to idols." His heart was
set on his idols. When the heart is set on things, it loves
them. You know that Samuel told Saul not to set his
heart on his father's donkeys (1 Sam. 9:20). Men's hearts
are set on their goods, their cattle, their corn, their wine
and oil, their pleasures and profits, and those things that
the world holds out to them. But Colossians 3:2 reminds
us: "Set your affections on things above, not on things
on the earth." Men settle their affections on the things
of earth. One thing or another here below steals away
their hearts, their hearts are taken up with them, and so
they love these things. Matthew 24:38 says, "For as in
the days that were before the flood they were eating and
drinking, marrying and giving in marriage." Their affections were set on those things. When our affections are
set on something, we love that thing.

5. We are said to love the world when we employ most
of our strength in, on, and about the things of the world.
When our chief strength is employed toward something, we commit our time and energy to it. "Labour not
for the meat which perisheth," said Christ, "but for that
meat which endureth unto everlasting life, which the
Son of man shall give unto you" (John 6:27).When our
chief labor concerns meat that perishes and other such
things, we love them. When the bent of the soul is that
way, there is love. When men rise early, lie down late,
and spend their time that way, it is out of love. Romans

13:14 reminds us to "make not provision for the flesh, to fulfil the lusts thereof." When we make provision for the flesh and its lusts — to fulfill them, to gratify them, and satisfy them — it is evident that we love the world. Men follow it with eagerness, and their time and strength are spent that way.

6. We are said to love the world when we watch all opportunities and occasions to get the things of the world: to buy cheap and sell high; to get great estates, houses, lands, and things of that nature. "The children of this world," said Christ, "are in their generation wiser than the children of light" (Luke 16:8). The children of the world are wise in their generation to get all advantages whereby to raise themselves. But, "hear this, O ye that swallow up the needy, even to make the poor of the land to fail" (Amos 8:4). They watched for opportunities to swallow up the needy, to make a prey of the needy, to have their labor for a song, or for nothing at all. They are like the eagle that soars aloft, looking down to seize its prey. The heart ranges and roves abroad, seeking after one thing or another in the world to settle on. Yet remember the words of our Lord: "Seek not ye what ye shall eat, or what ye shall drink, neither be ye of doubtful mind" (Luke 12:29). Do not be like meteors in the air that fall to the earth. So many are like meteors in the air, hovering about; at last they fall on the earth.

Some will say, "If I had gotten such an estate, then I could take my ease and be at rest." In Proverbs 18:11, the wise man says, "The rich man's wealth is his strong city, and as an high wall in his own conceit." When a rich man gets wealth, he will settle upon it. It is his strong city, and he will rest there. It is as a high wall in his own mind, thinking it will defend him against all enemies, injuries, and wrongs. So we love the world when we watch for advantages in order to confide in, trust in, and secure ourselves by them.

7. We love the world when we endure great hardships for it. We will endure most anything for that which we love. Jacob loved Rachel, so he endured cold and heat, winter and summer, to accomplish his desires. So when men endure great difficulties, run through great dangers, and venture upon anything to get the world, they can be said to love it. It is said of our soldiers that they will risk their limbs and lives for pennies a day. And there are businessmen who will venture their souls for their credit. They do not consider it to be their credit or honor to put up with an injury or a wrong, but they will hazard their lives and souls to maintain their credit and honor. In Psalm 107:23–27 you may see how men endure the danger and storms at sea:

> They that go down to the sea in ships, that do business in the great waters; these see the works of the LORD, and his wonders in the deep. For he commandeth, and raiseth the stormy wind, which lifteth up the waves thereof. They mount up to

the heaven, they go down again to the depths:
their soul is melted because of trouble.

They endure trouble that melts their very souls. "They
reel to and fro and stagger like a drunken man, and are
at their wit's end." Men will endure anything at sea to
get the wealth of the world, which suggests they love the
world. No amount of difficulties will quench their love;
though they meet with storms and waves and danger,
yet their love for the world is not extinguished. Nothing
wearies them so long as they can get the world. But as
for the things of God and the soul, the gospel and the
Sabbath, how soon are men weary of these! Consider
again Amos 8:4–5:

> Hear this, O ye that swallow up the needy, even
> to make the poor of the land to fail, saying,
> When will the new moon be gone, that we may
> sell corn? and the sabbath, that we may set forth
> wheat, making the ephah small, and the shekel
> great, and falsifying the balances by deceit?

They are not weary of the world, yet they soon weary
of the Sabbath and the ordinances of God. Men can
endure any difficulty and danger to get estates, but they
will hardly endure anything to get heaven, grace, or an
interest in Christ.

8. Men love the world when they favor the world the
most. When they most favor the things of the world
in their discourses, they are in love with the world.

Christ tells you, "Out of the abundance of the heart the mouth speaketh" (Matt. 12:34). When the world is in the heart, the heart loves it. Now it is evidence that the world is in the heart when our conversations are about the world and favor it most. In John 3:31, the Lord Christ says, "He that cometh from above is above all: he that is of the earth is earthly, and speaketh of the earth." Earthly people favor the things of the earth in their speech. How savory discussions of gain, pleasures, and honors are to them. And in John 8:23 we read, "And he said unto them, Ye are from beneath; I am from above: ye are of this world; I am not of this world." Christ was not of the world, and He was ever speaking of heaven and heavenly things — the things that concern the eternal good of men's souls. They, however, were of the earth and spoke of the earth. Jesus referred to the scribes and Pharisees as ones who loved the applause of men and sought places of honor. They were of the earth; therefore, they savored the things of the earth and spoke of them much. Yet Christ was of heaven and spoke of heavenly things. They were minding their cumin, anise, mint, and tithes, while neglecting the weighty things of the Law. Their hearts were on those things.

It says in 1 John 4:5: "They are of the world; there-fore speak they of the world, and the world heareth them." Men are of the world, and people love to hear them speak of the world. But when any speak of heav-enly things, how unwelcome and unsavory are they?

"The natural man receiveth not the things of the Spirit of God: for they are foolishness unto him: neither can he know them, because they are spiritually discerned" (1 Cor. 2:14). They do not perceive the things of God, nor do they receive the things of God; such things are spiritual, and therefore are unwelcome to them. Therefore in Romans 8:5 the apostle says, "They that are after the flesh do mind the things of the flesh." They favor them, savor them, relish them, and delight in them. "But they that are after the Spirit [mind] the things of the Spirit." Isaiah 58:13 says:

> If thou turn away thy foot from the sabbath, from doing thy pleasure on my holy day; and call the sabbath a delight, the holy of the LORD, honourable; and shalt honour him, not doing thine own ways, nor finding thine own pleasure, nor speaking thine own words.

God accounts someone a gracious, heavenly, and good person if instead of forsaking the Sabbath, he turns away from finding pleasure in his own will and words. Now our own words are the words of the world; the words of the flesh. It seems to demonstrate that a man is not of the world when he savors the things of God and does not turn his feet away from the Sabbath, but rather turns from doing his own pleasure on God's holy day. But when we relish and savor the things of the world in our conversations, this shows we are glued to the world and love it.

9. A man loves the world when he mourns and laments for the things of the world that are taken from him. That which we love, we mourn over when we lose it. When men mourn exceedingly for a child, it shows that they loved their child. When men mourn and are afflicted for the loss of estate, names, friends, or relations, it shows that they loved the world. Rachel wept and refused to be comforted. Why? She had no children. How greatly are many people afflicted when they lose outward things such as credit, profit, honors, pleasures, estates, or relations. How they mourn and are discontent, hang down their head, and will not be comforted. They love the world and the things of the world.

10. We are said to love the world when we are resolved to be rich and will have the world one way or another. They will have the world by hook or by crook, as we used to say. First Timothy 6:9 speaks of "they that will be rich." They are resolved to be rich and to have the world, whatever comes of it. These men love the world indeed.

Now you see what the world is, and what it means to love it.

CHAPTER 2

Reasons for Not Loving the World

Why should we not love the world or the things of the world? There are many good reasons not to do so. Here are several to consider.

A Higher Calling

Those who are in a state of grace — be they babes, little children, young men, or fathers — should not love the world because they are called out of the world and destined for another. They are called to another state, to a state of grace. Their love should run toward grace and the things of that other world to which they are called. They are called to be heirs with Christ and of heaven, glory, and happiness. Therefore they should not love the world.

It Is Unreasonable

We should not love the world because it will direct us toward things that are unreasonable, which will be seen in these four particulars:

1. It will direct you to things that are merely probable, and make you leave things that are certain. It is unreasonable to be taken away from things that are certain in order to be put on things that are only probable. It is only probable for any man in this world to get the world. It is unreasonable to follow hard after that which is only probable, whether we shall get it or not. Haggai 1:6 says, "Ye have sown much, and bring in little; ye eat, but ye have not enough; ye drink, but ye are not filled with drink; ye clothe you, but there is none warm; and he that earneth wages earneth wages to put it into a bag with holes." Verse 9 then concludes, "Ye looked for much, and, lo, it came to little; and when ye brought it home, I did blow upon it."

It is a hazard, a great venture to get the things of this world. Men may take a great deal of pains to pursue these things eagerly, and yet come short of them. Most people die in their expectations; they look to get these things and do not get them. Indeed, those who labor most usually attain least. Therefore, as the wise man says in Ecclesiastes 9:11, "I returned, and saw under the sun, that the race is not to the swift." Now who should win the race but the swift? It is most probable that the swift should win the race; but "the race is not to the swift, nor the battle to the strong, neither yet bread to the wise, nor yet riches to men of understanding, nor yet favour to men of skill; but time and chance happeneth to them all." It is uncertain whether they shall get these things or not. The promises of the world and the devil are seldom made good. However, there are other things that are certain, and therefore it misleads men to think unreasonably to leave certain things for improbable things. God's promises are certain. God will not fail men who take pains for true wisdom and understanding. "Ask, and it shall be given you; seek, and ye shall find; knock, and it shall be opened unto you" (Matt. 7:7). Seek these things, for they are certain.

2. Supposing we do get the world with our endeavors, we cannot keep it without fear of losing it. Consider Proverbs 23:5: "Wilt thou set thine eyes upon that which is not? For riches certainly make themselves wings; they fly away as an eagle towards heaven." And consider too Proverbs 27:1: "Boast not thyself of to morrow; for thou knowest not what a day may bring forth." Tomorrow may bring a great storm, which may blow down the house; a great tempest, and the ship may be overturned or driven on an anchor and lose all the goods. Tomorrow there may be a fire in your house. Why, then, will you set your eyes on that which is not? But if we get grace, that will continue with us. If we get peace and joy, none can take them from us. If we get an interest in Christ, none can pluck us out of His hand.

3. Supposing we do get the things of the world and are able to keep them, they will not satisfy our souls. Therefore, it is unreasonable to let go of that which

will satisfy the soul in order to seek that which will not satisfy. Remember the words of Ecclesiastes 5:10: "He that loveth silver shall not be satisfied with silver." If we love the world — the honors, the pleasures, or anything in the world — we will not be satisfied with it. This is because everything has a crack in it; yes, there is a curse that goes along with it. Micah 6:14–15 says:

> Thou shalt eat, but not be satisfied; and thy casting down shall be in the midst of thee; and thou shalt take hold, but shalt not deliver; and that which thou deliverest will I give up to the sword. Thou shalt sow, but thou shalt not reap; thou shalt tread the olives, but thou shalt not anoint thee with oil; and sweet wine, but shalt not drink wine.

Every creature contains a vacuum, an emptiness that will not produce satisfaction. Nothing will yield that which we expect from it and look to it for. The satisfaction that we expect in riches, honors, trades, health, wives, children, or estates is not really there. Haman had great honor in the world, as much as a man could desire. Yet he lacked Mordecai's respect, and that soured everything for Haman (Esth. 5:9–14). There is vanity and vexation in all conditions of life. Solomon wrote that inscription on all things here in the world: "Vanity of vanities…all is vanity and vexation of spirit" (Eccl. 1:2, 14). Therefore, to love the world and the things of it directs us to unreasonable things. However, the things of God are better than the things of the world.

4. Loving the world directs us toward the worst things. All the things in the world are perishing, but the things of God are durable. The things of the world are but dog's meat; however, the things of God, heaven, and the kingdom are excellent things. There is an excellency in grace; there is an excellency in the knowledge of Christ. To let these things go and choose the others is unreasonable.

It Is Scandalous

We should not love the world because it is scandalous to the ways and things of God. When professing Christians are like the men of the world, their love for the world and the things of the world causes the appearance that they have nothing but a profession of religion. Truly, this is a scandal. In 2 Timothy 3:5, we read of those "having a form of godliness, but denying the power thereof." Who are those who have a form of godliness but deny the power? They are "covetous" men and "lovers of pleasures more than lovers of God" (2 Tim. 3:2, 4). This brings a great scandal on the ways of God, so much so that men of the world say, "These professing Christians are as covetous as any; they love the world as much as any; they are as greedy after the things of the world as any — what is in their religion?" Such hypocrisy causes religion to suffer. Like the spies who brought an ill report from the land of Canaan, which flowed with milk and honey, these mere worldly professors bring an ill report about God and His ordinances. Men of the world are ready to say, "So and so make great professions and make a great noise in the world, but silver comes from them as a joint from the body and as blood from their veins. They are so cheap that there is nothing to be gotten from them." So we read in Matthew 18:7: "Woe unto the world because of offences!" And one of the great offenses comes from professing Christians because they love the world so much.

It Is Idolatrous

As loving the world is scandalous, so it is also idolatrous. When men love the world, they make an idol of the world. The world has their hearts; their hearts are glued to it. Ephesians 5:5 states that the "covetous man…is an idolater." And in Colossians 3:5, Paul tells us that "covetousness…is idolatry." We cry out against Roman Catholics that they set up images and bow to them; yet we are greater idolaters ourselves if we love the world and the things of the world. We set up idols and pictures in our hearts; certainly idolatry is a great sin, and an idolater is a grievous sinner. We would hate to have the title of being idolaters fastened to us. Yet, if we love the world, we are idolaters and live in idolatry.

It Is Dangerous

It is a dangerous thing to love the world. A man who loves the world, whose bent is that way, is in danger of these things:

1. A man who loves the world grows, little by little, to be a stranger to God and Christ. We cannot simultaneously have our eyes on both heaven and earth. Suppose we are between two men or two mountains; the nearer we draw to one, the further we go from the other. So the further we go from God, the more we love the world. When men love the cistern, they leave the fountain. All creatures are but cisterns, and when our hearts run out to these, then we leave God, who is the fountain.

2. Another evil is that we grow acquainted with the world's ways and the ways of worldlings. We grow acquainted with their tricks and schemes, and many times with their oaths and wicked behavior. This over acquaintance defiles us and leaves us hardened to the things of God.

3. We expose ourselves to various temptations and snares which are hurtful. Those who long to be rich fall into snares, temptations, and many hurtful lusts. The odds are a thousand to one that we lose a good conscience by loving the world. No, we are in danger of losing our very souls by it. As we see in Matthew 19:23: "Then said Jesus unto his disciples, Verily I say unto you, That a rich man shall hardly enter into the kingdom of heaven." What danger is that man in who loves the world and the things of the world? He is in danger of losing heaven. "For what is a man profited, if he shall gain the whole world, and lose his own soul?" (Matt.

16:26). He who loves the world is laboring to get the world and to be great in the world, and so he hazards his soul. It is dangerous to love the world.

It Deals with the Impossible

We should not love the world because it puts us on impossibilities. As we read in Matthew 6:24: "No man can serve two masters: for either he will hate the one, and love the other; or else he will hold to the one, and despise the other. Ye cannot serve God and mammon." The Lord Jesus Christ tells you that it is an impossibility to serve God and wealth. Every man says, "I will serve God and love Him. I would not be worthy to live otherwise." But if we love the world, we do not serve or love God. We cannot serve both the riches of the world and the Lord God; it is an impossible thing. Therefore, the Lord Christ, when He was tempted by the devil in Matthew 4:10, said, "Get thee hence, Satan: for it is written, Thou shalt worship the Lord thy God, and him only shalt thou serve." That is, "I cannot listen to your temptations to embrace the world, Satan. No, it is impossible, for I will serve God alone." God alone should be served, and we cannot serve two masters. Whoever loves the world has two masters to serve, God and the world, and it is impossible to serve them both.

It Makes God Our Enemy

We should not love the world because it makes God our enemy. It was a sad thing when God said to Jerusalem,

"Behold, I am against thee" (Jer. 21:13). That is to say, "I am your enemy." How dreadful it is to have the great God — the Lord of Hosts, the Lord of Sabbaths, the Lord of Heaven and Earth — to be our enemy! Whoever loves the world is the enemy of God. James 4:4 says, "Ye adulterers and adulteresses, know ye not that the friendship of the world is enmity with God?" Do you desire to be God's enemy? Love the world. If you do not want to be an enemy of God, do not love the world. It is better to have the entire world as our enemy than for God to be against us. In Psalm 10:3 it speaks of "the covetous, whom the LORD abhorreth." A man with a covetous heart is greedy for the world, and God abhors him. To have God as our enemy is sad. What will become of that man or woman who has God for his or her enemy? The love of the world makes God our enemy.

It Is a Waste of Time

We should not love the world because it makes us waste our time, which is better than the world. Would any man lay out gold and silver for straws, stubble, chips, butterflies, and such things as these? Those who love the world are worth more than the world, and they give that for the world which is better than the world. The best things of the world are its riches, learning, and gifts. But our souls are better than all these, better than the whole world. "What shall a man give in exchange for his soul?" (Matt. 16:26). The whole world is not worth one soul;

one soul is worth a million worlds. Now in laying out our time, strengths, understandings, and souls for the world and the things of the world, what expenses have we paid? We give too much for the world. The world is not worthy of our affections, understandings, strengths, and hearts. Therefore, see what the prophet said in Isaiah 55:2. He comes there with a vehement complaint: "Wherefore do ye spend money for that which is not bread?" It is not bread when you get it. It is not anything that will satisfy or in any way bring an advantage to your souls. And you spend "your labour for that which satisfieth not." So we are at too great a cost and at too great an expense when we love the world. We labor to get the world and buy it at so dear a rate.

It Debases Our Understanding

We should not love the world because it debases the understanding, that most noble faculty of the soul. The world debases our minds, and for what? The world is a mere, dirty thing. Romans 8:20–21 shows that the world is "subject to vanity" and held under "the bondage of corruption." Likewise, 1 John 5:19 says that "the whole world lieth in wickedness." It lies like a piece of rotting carcass in a ditch; it lies in the wicked one, in the devil. And what can the world contribute to your understanding that will do you good? No, it debases the minds and makes the soul earthy, drossy, muddy, and miry. Now, will you debase a noble soul for a dirty world? In Daniel 2, mention is made of a great image. And what was the best part of that image? The feet were clay, the legs were iron, the thighs were brass, the belly was silver, and the head was gold. The best part was but gold and silver, and those are rusty, perishing things; it debases a noble, heroic soul to be bowed down to these things. The soul becomes what it loves. If it loves the earth, it is an earthy soul.

It Is Utterly Destructive

The world is of a damning nature, and therefore we should not love it. The world not only endangers us, but it drowns the soul in perdition. It says in 1 Timothy 6:9, "They that will be rich fall into temptation and a snare, and into many foolish and hurtful lusts, which drown men in destruction and perdition." The soul is drowned in utter ruin. Whoever is a lover of the world is a child of the world, and so is a son of perdition. It is said of the "man of sin" that he is a "son of perdition" (2 Thess. 2:3). The world makes men leave Christ. In Matthew 19:16–22, a young man came to Christ and asked, "Good Master, what good thing shall I do, that I may have eternal life?" Christ said, "Keep the commandments." The young man said to Him, "Which?" Jesus said, "Thou shalt do no murder, thou shalt not commit adultery," etc. The young man replied to Him, "All these things have I kept from my youth up: what lack I yet?" Jesus responded to him, "If thou wilt be perfect, go and sell that thou hast, and give to the poor, and thou shalt have treasure in heaven: and come and follow me." But he left Christ. "He went away sorrowful," the text says. Why? "He had great possessions." The scribes and Pharisees left Christ for their reputation among men (John 12:42–43). So in Matthew 8:34, the Gadarenes (or Gergesenes, KJV) desired Christ to be gone out of their country; they would have none of Him. They loved their swine which were drowned in the sea, and the world drowned them in perdition.

It Is Hostile to Godliness

The world is a great enemy to growth in grace and communion with God, for the things of the world divert the heart from spiritual things. Martha was encumbered about many things and diverted from Christ and hearing Him. So Matthew 13:22: "He also that received seed among the thorns is he that heareth the word; and the care of this world, and the deceitfulness of riches, choke the word, and he becometh unfruitful." So the love of the world and the things of the world are a great enemy to godliness. It makes men leave the best things, the most excellent things, even grace itself, God Himself, and communion with God. A worldly heart has little or no communion with God. If a wife falls in love and commits folly with someone that is not her husband, her husband will no longer care for communion with her. And so it is in James 4:4: "Ye adulterers and adulteresses, know ye not that the friendship of the world is enmity with God? Whosoever therefore will be a friend of the world is the enemy of God." Psalm 73:27 speaks of "them that go a whoring from thee [God]." Men go a whoring from God when they love the world and dote on the things of it. See what an enemy the world is to growth in grace and communion with God!

It Is the Devil's Trap
The world is the devil's instrument whereby he ensnares men and women and leads them captive at his pleasure. In 2 Corinthians 4:4, Satan is called "the god of this world," and the world is his grand instrument to take men and women. In Matthew 4:8–9, the devil tried to catch Christ with the glory of the world: "The devil taketh him up into an exceeding high mountain, and sheweth him all the kingdoms of the world, and the glory of them." Here was his last bait by which he thought he could catch Christ. "And saith unto him, All these things will I give thee, if thou wilt fall down and worship me." He attempted to catch Christ with it, but the Lord Christ was too hard for him. Nevertheless, it is his instrument whereby he catches mere men and women. Thus he caught Eve by the fruit of the garden. Thus he caught David by Bathsheba. Thus he caught Achan by a wedge of gold and a garment. And thus he catches men and women today, some by wine, some by women, and some by kingdoms. The devil leads them

captive when he has taken them by some worldly bait. He presents one thing or another that is suitable to the eye, to the taste, to the fancy, or to their opinion. He presents something suitable by which he leads them captive at his will.

It Leads to Apostasy

We should not love the world because it causes men to err and go astray from the ways of God, leading them to apostasy in the end. It says in 1 Timothy 6:10: "The love of money is the root of all evil: which while some coveted after, they have erred from the faith." Mark it well; they have erred from the faith. If we love the world, we will let the faith go, the truth go, and the ways of God go — and so we make way for apostasy. Love of the world, esteem among men in the world, and outward engagements with the things of the world cause people to renounce the faith. And so it was with Demas in 2 Timothy 4:10: "Demas hath forsaken me, having loved this present world." What? Forsake the great apostle Paul for the present world? Yet Demas did it. The love of the world drew him away from Paul, Paul's teachings, and Paul's ways. So you see the reasons why we should not love the world and the things of the world.

CHAPTER 3

Our Relationship to God's Creation

Several questions arise at this point. In answering them, we will better see how we relate to God's creation.

How to Relate to the World

If we are not to love the world, must we then totally cast off the world and have nothing to do with it? The answer is no. It does not say that we may not have anything to do with the world, but that we must not love the world. Surely we have something to do with the world. I shall answer this question more fully by discussing several areas where we have legitimate interaction with the world.

1. *We may study the world and the works of God in the world.* They are honorable, "sought out of all them that have pleasure therein" (Ps. 111:2). We may study the world, for the world will teach us many good lessons.

Studying the visible things of the world brings knowledge of the invisible things of God: "For the invisible things of him from the creation of the world are clearly seen, being understood by the things that are made, even his eternal power and Godhead; so that they are without excuse" (Rom. 1:20). We may come to know that there is an eternal and omnipotent God by these visible things: "But ask now the beasts, and they shall teach thee; and the fowls of the air, and they shall tell thee: or speak to the earth, and it shall teach thee: and the fishes of the sea shall declare unto thee" (Job 12:7–8). The beasts, the birds, the earth, and the fish will teach us of the invisible things of God. Instruction in those things may do us good. Because there is something to be learned from them, we may pursue them in study. God's power, wisdom, goodness, and mercy are all learned from God's creation.

Creation teaches us prudence and providence. "Go to the ant, thou sluggard" (Prov. 6:6). Even it lays up a store in summer against winter.

Creation will teach us to do the will of God. "They continue this day according to thine ordinances: for all are thy servants" (Ps. 119:91). They all serve God. The sun, moon, and stars all serve the Lord. Even the winds serve the Lord, for God's Word speaks of the "stormy wind fulfilling his word" (Ps. 148:8). When the very winds fulfill the Word of God, obey His voice, and do what He commands them to do, they teach us therefore to do the will of God. Shall the waves, winds, and all of creation obey the Lord, while man stands in disobedience to the Lord? Man, too, was created for the Lord.

Creation teaches us to wait on God. "The eyes of all wait upon thee; and thou givest them their meat in due season" (Ps. 145:15). The birds of the air and the creatures of the sea wait on God for food. Will we be anxious and distressed about what we will eat, what we will drink, and how we will be clothed, when God feeds the wild fowl in the air? The Lord feeds them; therefore, they teach us to wait on God without desponding and becoming distracted with worries.

Creation teaches us to expect glorious liberty from the hand of God. Romans 8:19 reminds us that "the earnest expectation of the creature waiteth for the manifestation of the sons of God." And verse 21 says that they wait to be "delivered from the bondage of corruption into the glorious liberty of the children of God." The children of God can come to a glorious liberty. They may be in bondage, and are at this day, but there is a glorious liberty. Shall we not wait for it when the whole creation waits for it?

Creation teaches us to know times and seasons. The stork, the crane, and the swallow know their times and seasons, and shall we not know them too? We are therefore to make it a part of our learning to study the world as God's creation.

2. *We may pray for the things of this world.* In Proverbs 30:8 Agur prays, "Remove far from me vanity and lies: give me neither poverty nor riches; feed me with food convenient for me." You see here that he prays for con-

venient food. So in Luke 11:3 Christ teaches us to pray, "Give us day by day our daily bread." That is, grant us those things needful for this life — needful for my condition and the relations that I am in.

3. *We must follow a calling in this world.* God calls us to use lawful means to obtain the things of the world. Consider what Paul told the Thessalonians, "If any would not work, neither should he eat.... Now them that are such we command and exhort by our Lord Jesus Christ, that with quietness they work, and eat their own bread" (2 Thess. 3:10–12). The Lord commands men to have a calling and to be diligent in it. First Corinthians 7:33 describes how the man "that is married careth for the things that are of the world, how he may please his wife." He ought to take care to please his wife and provide for his family. As 1 Timothy 5:8 reminds us, "if any provide not for his own, and specially for those of his own house, he hath denied the faith, and is worse than an infidel." Furthermore, we ought to labor so that we have the resources to relieve others: "Let him that stole steal no more: but rather let him labour, working with his hands the thing which is good, that he may have to give to him that needeth" (Eph. 4:28). Men should try to follow a calling so that they will not have to live off of others and be idle. We should strive to have enough to meet people's needs and help others who are impotent, aged, sick, weak, or made poor by the providence of God. Acts 20:35 says, "It is more blessed to give than to

receive." Men should labor therefore to have enough so that they may give rather than receive.

4. *We may use the world.* Our text does not say, "Do not use the world." Rather, it tells us not to love the world or the things of it. Notice how 1 Corinthians 7:31 speaks of people "that use this world, as not abusing it." Men indeed abuse the world to gratify their lusts and satisfy the flesh, as in 1 John 2:16: "For all that is in the world, the lust of the flesh, and the lust of the eyes, and the pride of life, is not of the Father, but is of the world." We may use the world, but not abuse it.

How to Use It Rightly

When does a man so use the world as not to abuse it? Here are six basic ways that we can use God's creation well and right.

1. *Use all things for the end that God has made them.* In Proverbs 16:4 you see God's purpose for making the world: "The LORD hath made all things for himself." God made everything in the world for Himself, for His own praise, honor, and glory. And therefore 1 Corinthians 10:31 says: "Whether therefore ye eat, or drink, or whatsoever ye do, do all to the glory of God." Let God be glorified in your eating and drinking, in your recreations, in all your actions, in all your sufferings; do all to the glory of God, for God "hath made all things for himself." Furthermore, 1 Corinthians 6:20 reminds us: "Ye are

bought with a price: therefore glorify God in your body, and in your spirit, which are God's." When you use your mind, your affections, your speech, your eyes, your hands, your feet; when you run in the way of God's commandments; when you use all for the glory of God — then you do not abuse the world, but use it the right way.

2. *Walk with God in the use of the world and answer God's call.* It is said that Enoch walked with God three hundred years; he walked with God in his calling. We are but stewards, and God calls on us now and then to do one thing or another. He calls us to give to the poor, so we answer God's call. When God calls us to mourn, we mourn. When He calls us to sympathize with those who suffer, we sympathize. When He calls us to rejoice, we rejoice. When we abridge our liberty at God's call, then we use the world aright.

3. *Use the things of the world to promote spiritual good in ourselves and others.* "And we know that all things work together for good to them that love God, to them who are the called according to his purpose" (Rom. 8:28). When I use the world to promote my spiritual life, get more grace, and further my peace, comfort, contentment, and communion with God, I use the world aright and well. "Let your light so shine before men, that they may see your good works, and glorify your Father which is in heaven" (Matt. 5:16). When I use the world so that I make my light to shine by it, and so to shine that men

may see my good works; when I do good with my estate, so that men may glorify God — then I use my property correctly. Making friends with unrighteous mammon is not using the world properly and does not promote spiritual good. Many use their material resources to crush others, get revenge, and have their lusts satisfied; and so they promote the interest of Satan. This is an ill use of the world and the things of the world.

4. *Use the world slightly and consider the things of God and of my soul as my main business.* Why has God set me in this world? Is it to get riches and honors, to have pleasures and gratify my lusts? No, it is to glorify His name and work out my own salvation. Now when I make this my main business, I use the world aright. Therefore Christ said, "Labour not for the meat which perisheth, but for that meat which endureth unto everlasting life, which the Son of man shall give unto you: for him hath God the Father sealed" (John 6:27). Let it be your main business to get the bread that endures to everlasting life. Seek grace, work out your salvation, get assurance and clear evidences for an eternal good condition. This pursuit must be your main job here in the world. But many look at heaven and the things of God as secondary things, looking after the world as the main business.

5. *Use the world in moderation, keeping your affections in check.* We should hold the world lightly in our hands, as if it were not in our grasp. And this you shall see plainly

in 1 Corinthians 7:29–31: "it remaineth, that both they that have wives be as though they had none." I rightly use the world when my affection toward my wife is moderated so as not to take her for granted. "And they that rejoice, as though they rejoiced not." Do you have prosperous times, when all things go well? Rejoice in a way that shows that these times are not your ultimate source of joy. "And they that buy, as though they possessed not." Do not be so attached to your possessions, houses, and lands when you purchase them. "And they that use this world, as not abusing it." Let our moderation be toward things as if they were not ultimately ours. Indeed, "let your moderation be known unto all men" (Phil. 4:5).

6. *Give a good and cheerful account to God concerning what we have had in the world.* God gives some men great portions and some men less portions; everyone has something. We must use our gifts, our resources, and our relations so that we can give a good account to God. It will be said before long to every man and woman, "You have had a spouse, children, parents, brothers and sisters, health, strength, and the like. Come, give an account of your stewardship." When we so use the things we have in this world that we can give a good and cheerful account to God, we have not abused the world but used it in the right way.

Loving Good Things

Some may still ask the following questions: Are not God's creatures good, and may we not love them as good? Is not good the object of love? These are good questions, and the following points will help us resolve their underlying concern.

1. *Keep the good of creation in proper perspective.* The good in the creature is very, very little compared to spiritual good or the goodness of God. The good of the creature is very little, and so little that it cannot make us good. Rather it tends to further our corruptions and feed our lust, for "all that is in the world" is considered "the lust of the flesh, and the lust of the eyes, and the pride of life" (1 John 2:16). The things of the world feed our lusts and are stronger to set our corruptions to work than to further the good that is in us. And because the things of the world divert us from God, discourage us toward good, or corrupt the good that is in us, therefore the Lord has forbidden us to love the world — even though there is some good in the world.

2. *Remember the right use of these good things.* We may love the world and the things thereof as a man loves the tools he uses to carry out his business. That is, we may love the world as it may further us in our chief business. As far as riches can be used to promote and further our spiritual interest in Christ — our peace, comfort, and graces — so far we may love the world.

3. *Place the greatest Good second to none.* We may love the world with a subordinate love to God, so long as it does not hinder our love for God. In this way we may love the good that is in the world and in the creature. Otherwise, we must not love the world.

Recognizing Our Reward

May someone follow a particular calling in life for the purpose of being rich or accept a job because it will bring in most gain? Men do live and have their callings in the world. Therefore, would it not make sense that they should labor to be profitable in the riches of this world? Although making wealth one's goal is a common practice of men, the simple answer is that they may not do so. Here are five reasons that should help explain this answer:

1. *It is a heathenish thing to argue for the goodness of a calling from the gain of a calling.* In Acts 19:24–25, we read how "a certain man named Demetrius, a silversmith, which made silver shrines for Diana, brought no small gain unto the craftsmen; whom he called together with the workmen of like occupation, and said, Sirs, ye know that by this craft we have our wealth." The heathens argued for the goodness of their calling from the gain that it brought to them. Now we should not consider a calling good because it is profitable; the very heathens did so. Thus, 2 Peter 2:3 speaks of false prophets: "Through covetousness shall they with feigned words

make merchandise of you." True prophets should have been supported and encouraged enough to live comfortably, but the end of their calling was not gain. The Scripture condemns it, and it was their sin; they would sell their souls for gain. They did not care what became of their souls so long as they might have gain and profit.

When two callings in life lie before someone, that person should not choose between them based on which will bring the most gain. Rather, a person must choose the calling that fits them best. God gives us gifts and talents for doing good to others and glorifying Him, and that is what should influence our decision.

2. *We must aim at the public good in our callings.* We work for the good of the church and the good of the state, not for our personal gain. "When Sanballat the Horonite, and Tobiah the servant, the Ammonite, heard of it, it grieved them exceedingly that there was come a man to seek the welfare of the children of Israel" (Neh. 2:10). Nehemiah did not seek himself; he sought the public good. He was called to be governor and he sought the welfare of the children of Israel. In Esther 10:3 it is said of Mordecai that he was "accepted of the multitude of his brethren, seeking the wealth of his people, and speaking peace to all his seed." So everyone should make it their main goal to seek the public good of church or state. As a heathen said, "Our country, parents, and friends challenge part of our estates, callings, or what we get; we are not to be for ourselves, but for the public

good." So in 2 Corinthians 12:15 the apostle says, "I will very gladly spend and be spent for you; though the more abundantly I love you, the less I be loved." Paul would sacrifice himself if there were occasion to strengthen their faith or do them good. That is how far he was from seeking himself in his calling.

3. *To make being rich our goal is against that great and glorious principle of the gospel, self-denial.* In Matthew 16:24 our blessed Savior said, "If any man will come after me, let him deny himself, and take up his cross, and follow me." He must deny himself. Now if I deny myself, I cannot set myself up at the same time. And Paul complained about this in Philippians 2:21: "All seek their own, not the things which are Jesus Christ's." Every man is for himself — his own honor, profit, and pleasure — and does not deny himself. Self-denial is a great and glorious truth that every man and woman should take notice of and put in practice, else they are not the disciples of the Lord Christ.

4. *It is directly against Scripture for us to make earthly gain our end.* "Labour not to be rich" (Prov. 23:4). That must not be your goal. Most men labor to be rich and great in the world, but these should not be their ends. To labor to be rich is directly against John 6:27: "Labour not for the meat which perisheth, but for that meat which endureth unto everlasting life." We should make everlasting life our goal, not things that perish.

5. *We should follow our calling to glorify God, whether we get any gain or not.* God placed Adam in a calling so that he might glorify Him. "Whether therefore ye eat, or drink, or whatsoever ye do, do all to the glory of God" (1 Cor. 10:31). We should aim for God's glory in our callings. In Ephesians 6:5–8, speaking of servants in their calling, Paul says, "Servants, be obedient to them that are your masters according to the flesh, with fear and trembling, in singleness of your heart, as unto Christ." They must serve and glorify Christ in their callings, regardless of their low status. The lowest servant should serve Christ, "not with eyeservice, as menpleasers; but as the servants of Christ, doing the will of God from the heart; with good will doing service, as to the Lord, and not to men." They should not be men-pleasers or seek themselves, but serve the Lord. They should seek to honor the Lord, "knowing that whatsoever good thing any man doeth, the same shall he receive of the Lord, whether he be bond or free." We will receive a reward from the Lord if we are right in our callings, not making gain and profit to be our aim and end.

CHAPTER 4

Applications of the Doctrine

I now come to the uses of the point, that those who are in a state of grace — whether they are little children, young men, or fathers — ought not to love the world or the things of it. I will also give some directions for examining our hearts for the love of the world.

Its Usefulness

Use 1. This informs us of the corruption of our natures, which are very prone to love the world and the things of the world. Therefore God gives a flat prohibition, "Love not the world, neither the things that are in the world" (1 John 2:15). This prohibition suggests that men and women since the Fall are most inclined to love the creature, for in their fall they left the Creator to run to the creature. And we are so turned to things that we idolize them, dote on them, spend our time and strength on them, and forget God and the things of God. Water is not more prone to run downward, nor the fire to climb upwards, than our hearts are to chase after earthly things. This is common to all men, a universal sickness and disease in all. Our hearts and natures are exceedingly corrupt, being prone to these things that are forbidden. It should humble us that we are so corrupt and go the wrong way; that we mind poor, perishing, vain things, and neglect God Himself, who alone can say, "I am that I am. I am substance and being. I am excellency. I am worthy of love, and yet I am not beloved."

Use 2. If those in a state of grace should not love the world, it would seem that the number is very, very few who are truly in the state of grace; there are so few who do not love the world. The love of the world is so common that it proclaims to the world, "They have no grace, or only seeming grace; not saving grace." Paul said, "All seek their own, not the things which are Jesus Christ's" (Phil. 2:21). It was so in the apostles' days; men loved the world and the things of the world, the honors of the world, the preferences of the world, places of power, riches, pleasures, and things of that nature — things suitable to the flesh and the old man. They loved these things, and Christ was not regarded. As we see in Revelation 13:3, "all the world wondered after the beast." It is rare to find a man estranged from the world, who will live above the world. "Our conversation," said Paul, "is in heaven" (Phil. 3:20). Where are the people whose conversation is in heaven? Where are the ones who will say, "Our commonwealth is in heaven, we are citizens of heaven, our affections are in heaven, our trading is in heaven"? People like this are very rare to find.

Use 3. If such should not love the world, then those who are gracious and godly should be content with a little of the world. A little of the world should serve them well; a little will carry us to our journey's end. It is unwise to load ourselves with thick clay when we have a journey to take or a race to run. The apostle says in Hebrews 13:5: "Let your conversation be without covetousness; and be content with such things as ye have." You who are Christians, be content with such things as you have and do not covet the world and the things of the world. "We brought nothing into this world, and it is certain we can carry nothing out. And having food and raiment let us be therewith content" (1 Tim. 6:7–8). A gracious heart should reason like this: "I brought nothing into the world, and I will carry nothing out. So if I have food and raiment and things convenient for me while I am in the world, why should I trouble myself any further to toil and labor for I know not what?" Men do not consider the certainty that they will not carry anything out of the world, but it is certain. This foundation is so solid you can build on it: you will take nothing with you when you die. Well, let us be content then with a little of the world.

Use 4. This serves to reprove most men and women that are professing Christians, those who are looked at as godly and in the state of grace. It is a rebuke to them,

for there are so many in the church that love the world
and the things of the world. I might bitterly and sharply
reprove professing Christians on this account.

Examining Our Hearts

But I know what will be said immediately: "We do not
love the world, we only use the world!" I would be glad if
this proved to be the case, so let us try it out whether we
love the world or not. I will put some questions to your
hearts and ask you to deal impartially with them. For
you see what is said, "Love not the world, neither the
things that are in the world" (1 John 2:15). Ask your-
selves these questions:

*Am I more concerned about the things of the world than I
am for heaven and spiritual things?*

How careful men and women are for purchases
and good bargains, and what costs they bear for houses
and land! What pains men take about these things.
If there is an uncertainty in a title of land or a house,
they will take great pains to clear up matters and make
things sure. If a storm at sea puts ships in danger, what
insuring is there? Men will take pains and pay whatever
it costs to insure their goods, but they take little pains
and avoid the slightest cost associated with the eternal
condition of their souls. Whereas the Scripture says in
Philippians 2:12, "Work out your own salvation with
fear and trembling."

You are in a storm, and your salvation is in danger.
You may lose your soul, so work out your salvation with
fear and trembling. Work it out of the dark. Work it out
of doubts, fears, and all disputes. Work it out against
all objections, and get things cleared up. Work out your
salvation with fear and trembling. It is a hard work, a
difficult work to accomplish, and great pains must be
taken about it. "Give diligence to make your calling and
election sure" (2 Peter 1:10). There must be diligence, for
it is not easily done. Merely reciting "Lord, have mercy
upon me" will not save or assure a man. No, there must
be praying, struggling, crying, and wrestling with God.
One must search Scripture and apply its truths to his
own heart. So 2 Peter 1:5 speaks of "giving all diligence,
add to your faith virtue" and the like. Men and women
should be diligent, very diligent, and all their diligence
should be to get grace and to make their callings and
elections sure. We give all diligence in other things, yet
little pain is taken about the soul. What does such mis-
placed concern suggest but that you love the world?

*Does the world push aside and cut out the things that are of
God? Do the things of the world jostle the wall of the things
of God?*

In Luke 14:18–20, when guests were called to
the great feast, they all made their excuses. They said,
"I have bought a piece of ground, and I must needs go
and see it.... I have bought five yoke of oxen, and I go
to prove them.... I have married a wife, and therefore I

cannot come." They could not come to hear Christ, nor partake of the great things that Christ offered to them in the gospel. Even so the things of the world jostle our prayer, reading of the Word, instructing our family in meditation, and the examination of our hearts. And if the things of the world do not jostle spiritual matters out altogether, they curtail and diminish them.

We must seriously ask our hearts whether we seek the kingdom of God and His righteousness. The things of the world jostle out the things of the kingdom of heaven, the things of God, and the important matters of the soul. It is evidence that we love the world when we set aside things of greater weight and concern for petty things in comparison. Some slight business will make a man neglect holy duties, or perform them merely in a formal way, whereas David, who was a gracious man after God's own heart, said, "I thought on my ways, and turned my feet unto thy testimonies" (Ps. 119:59). That is, "I considered my ways; the world was drawing me another way, but I considered my ways and turned my feet toward Thy testimonies. I made haste and did not delay to keep Thy commandments." And a few verses later: "At midnight I will rise to give thanks unto thee because of thy righteous judgments" (Ps. 119:62). That is, "I will rise at midnight. I will break my sleep. I will do it in secret when no eye sees me, when none is privy to it but God." We hardly will awake to give thanks to God for choice mercies, much less for righteous judgments. Allowing spiritual things and duties to be thrust aside on account of the things of the world suggests that we love the world too much.

Am I content with a little when it comes to matters of the soul?

Are you content with a little grace, with a little knowledge of God, with a little communion with God, with a little heavenly mindedness? But are you not eager for the things of the world, and never content and satisfied with what you have of them? Would you not have more and more and more, and more still of the things of the world — more this week, more next year, and daily more and more of the world? Is your soul like the horse leech in Proverbs 30:15 that cries, "Give, give"? Soul, if it is so, you love the world.

Men and women deceive themselves into thinking that they do not love the world when they are greedy and covetous after the things of the world. This is reflected in Amos 8:5: "When will the new moon be gone, that we may sell corn? and the sabbath, that we may set forth wheat?" That is, "When will these spiritual duties be over so that we may mind the world, follow the world, and get the world?" As it says in Proverbs 1:19, "So are the ways of every one that is greedy of gain." Men are greedy of gain, looking on the rich and laboring to be like them. We want to be as great and high and honorable as they are, to make the great purchases that they do, to have as great revenues and incomes as they have. But we do not tend to look at those who are rich in grace, those who are very spiritual, heavenly, and godly, who walk closely with God, and say, "I wish I were like them," and so labor to get more grace and to walk with God as Enoch did for three hundred years. Now when it is thus, it suggests that we love the world. Ask your own heart therefore whether it is so with you. Do you desire more and more of the world, but do not desire more and more of heaven and God?

In what then do I find most sweetness and contentment?

Is your contentment in the world and the things that it offers? Surely they are sweet and pleasing to our natures. But what about the things of heaven? Are they like the white of an egg, unsavory things with little pleasure in their taste? There are many who say, "Who will show us any good? Who will show us a good bargain?" But David said, "LORD, lift thou up the light of thy countenance upon us" (Ps. 4:6). David found good in it; the light of God's countenance was sweet to him. He was able to exclaim: "O taste and see that the LORD is good" (Ps. 34:8). That is, "The Lord is good and very sweet to my soul." And he desired that others would taste how good the Lord is. He wanted them to have the favor of God, communion with God, peace with God, and joy in the Holy Ghost. Oh, these things have a sweet taste and relish to a gracious heart and soul!

Others say, "Who will show us any good, corn, wine, oil, pleasures, profits, and the like?" These are pleasing to them, while spiritual and heavenly things are but notions and shadows, and they make small account of them. But a gracious soul finds that "the statutes of the LORD are right, rejoicing the heart" (Ps. 19:8). David's crown and kingdom did not rejoice his heart as much as God's statutes did. As he said, "More to be desired are they than gold, yea, than much fine gold: sweeter also than honey and the honeycomb" (Ps. 19:10). Some say, "Give me gold, gold, gold!" But David would have us say, "The statutes of God are more desirable than fine gold, the choicest gold; they are sweeter than honey and the honeycomb." Honey is sweet, but the honeycomb is sweeter yet. Now what sweetness does your soul find in these things? A heart that loves the world says, "What profit is it that we have kept his ordinance, and that we have walked mournfully before the LORD of hosts?" (Mal. 3:14). That is, "We find no profit in serving God, praying much, reading, meditation, and holy conference with others. We find no profit in hearing the Word and worshiping God. What profit is it?" To such people, earthly gain is godliness; but to a gracious heart, anything of God is sweet and great gain.

Do I use questionable or unlawful means to get the world? Do I neglect lawful and unquestionable means that would get me heaven and spiritual things?

Many use questionable things, and unlawful ones too, to get the world. You have it in 1 Thessalonians 4:6: "That no man go beyond and defraud his brother in any matter: because that the Lord is the avenger of all such." Do not men take advantage of others and cheat them in order to get the world? Worldly men will oppress unsuspecting people, wringing and drawing from them in order to increase their own estates. Amos 8:5 speaks of people "falsifying the balances by deceit." When people use false weights, false ways, and false lights, it suggests that they love the world and the things of the world. They will hazard their souls and grate on their own consciences to get the world. If ever their consciences are awakened, they will speak, accuse, and condemn them for such practices. Surely we love the world if we can use questionable and unlawful means, and then neglect the means that are unquestionable and very lawful. God has appointed means to get grace: prayer, meditation, hearing the Word, and searching the Scriptures. These are means that are unquestionable and will bring in gain, whereas the others are questionable and unlawful means.

Do I love ideas, learning, wisdom of words, talents, gifts, and things of this nature?

All these things are of the world. And oh, how they tickle the fancies of men! Some men satisfy themselves with human learning, which shows they are but carnal, natural, and worldly. As Paul said in 1 Corinthians 2:4–5, "My speech and my preaching was not with the enticing words of man's wisdom, but in demonstration of the Spirit and of power: that your faith should not stand in the wisdom of men, but in the power of God."

Sadly, the faith of some stands in the wisdom of men, saying, "He is a fine orator; he is a learned man; he has singular notions and expressions." These things please them, yet they hardly welcome the simplicity of the gospel and plain wholesome truths. Now that which is of God is plain and spiritual, and the more spiritual any truth is, the more welcome to a gracious heart it is. But spiritual things become less acceptable to those that love the world, for they strike at their carnality and corruptions. So ask your heart about what charms it most.

Am I more grieved over the loss of outward, worldly things than I am for the loss of spiritual things?

Many mourn bitterly for husbands, wives, children, or homes that are taken away. They will often weep, hang down their heads, forsake their diet, stay in their beds, and will not be comforted. But if a godly minister is taken away, if ordinances are taken away, if a Sabbath is taken away, if religious meetings are taken away, who is troubled by such things? When we grieve more over the loss of things that we know we must part with than the loss of things concerning our souls, it is a good indication that we love the world.

Honestly answering these several questions should help you know whether you love the world or not. And if you find that your heart is set on this world, you are worthy of great blame.

CHAPTER 5

Further Motives for Not Loving the World

I urge you, stop loving the world and the things of the world. Stop loving the pomp and pleasures of the world — its profits, preferences, and honors. Here are several grounds or arguments to enforce this exhortation.

It Is Sinful

We should not love the world because it is a sin to love the world. Whatever is forbidden to us is a sin, and will you live in sin? Is sin a small matter? "Sin is the transgression of a law," you will say. Well, here is the law: "Love not the world." If you love the world, you transgress this law; therefore do not live in the transgression of this law. It is an ill thing to live in sin. Ezekiel 18:4 warns us that "the soul that sinneth, it shall die." Regardless of their souls' stature — whether the highest or lowest, learned or ignorant, rich or poor — if they live in sin they shall die. It is a dangerous thing to live in sin, no matter how pleasing, profitable, or honorable it may seem. And if you love the world, you live in sin. We should "abhor that which is evil; cleave to that which is good" (Rom. 12:9). The least sin is evil, even if it progresses no farther than a sinful thought or lust. And if it is evil even when it is not acted on, how much more evil is it if it is performed, lived in, and practiced? It will bring forth eternal death, "for the wages of sin is death" (Rom. 6:23).

God Commands against It

We should not love the world because it is the command of the great God. The great, blessed, and glorious God commands us to not love the world. "Love not the world, neither the things that are in the world" (1 John 2:15). Shall not the command of the great God prevail with us? In the word of a king there is power. Well, here is the word of the greatest King of all kings, the great God of heaven and earth: "Love not the world." Peter said, "Master, we have toiled all the night, and have taken nothing: nevertheless at thy word I will let down the net" (Luke 5:5). So we should hearken to the command of God. At Thy command, Lord, I will not love the world or the things that it offers.

Jeremiah 35:5 tells of some Rechabites whose father commanded them not to drink wine, plant vineyards, or build houses, and how Jeremiah set wine before them, saying, "Drink ye wine." They said in verses 6 and 7, "We will drink no wine: for Jonadab the son of Rechab our father commanded us, saying, Ye shall drink no wine, neither ye, nor your sons for ever: neither shall ye build house, nor sow seed, nor plant vineyard." Now see what the Lord said in verse 14: "The words of Jonadab the son of Rechab, that he commanded his sons not to drink wine, are performed." Now here are dutiful sons who observe the command of their father. They "are performed; for unto this day they drink none, but obey their father's commandment: notwithstanding I have spoken unto you, rising early and speaking; but ye hearkened not unto me." God is saying, "What a reproach this is to Me, that the command of a man is observed and obeyed, and My command, the great God who has your lives in My hand, is not observed or regarded."

Well, the great God says to us, "Love not the world." Therefore let His commands be of force and authority with us, to take our hearts off from the love of the world.

It Belongs to the Wicked

We should not love the world because it is the portion of wicked and ungodly men. Psalm 17:14 speaks of "men of the world, which have their portion in this life." There are people who are characterized by worldly principles, affections, practices, and livelihoods. They live for what this world can offer, and that is the extent of their gain. The things of this world are their portion. Would you have your reward here, in these things? It is a poor portion, a perishing portion, an unsatisfying portion, the worst portion of all.

In Job 21:7–13, Job asked, "Wherefore do the wicked live, become old, yea, are mighty in power?" Wicked men are not worthy to live in the world, yet they live long and are mighty in power, place, honor, and estates:

> Their seed is established in their sight with them, and their offspring before their eyes. Their houses are safe from fear, neither is the rod of God upon them. Their bull gendereth, and faileth not; their cow calveth, and casteth not her calf. They send forth their little ones like a flock, and their children dance. They take the timbrel and harp, and rejoice at the sound of the organ. They spend their days in wealth, and in a moment go down to the grave.

Here are wicked men; it is their portion to have the world, to have the music and mirth, and all things according to their hearts' desires. It is their portion, and who would not have such a portion? It was the troubled question of Jeremiah 12:1: "Wherefore doth the way of the wicked prosper?" Why are all of those who deal treacherously so happy? Wicked men prosper in the world. Though they deal treacherously, yet they prosper. And he says, "Thou hast planted them, yea, they have taken root: they grow, yea, they bring forth fruit: thou art near in their mouth, and far from their reins" (Jer. 12:2).

The wicked seek their reward in this world; therefore we should not love it. Alexander the Great, a heathen, had all the world for his portion. Julius Caesar had the Roman Empire for his portion. Ahasuerus had

127 provinces for his portion. The world is a portion fit for dogs, and is not children's meat. Therefore we should not love the world because it is the portion of the wicked.

It Only Disappoints

We should not love the world because it will only disappoint us. It gives us much trouble and little good. We are told that we will have great afflictions in the world. "In the world ye shall have tribulation" (John 16:33). The world is filled with thorny cares and piercing sorrows, and you will encounter them daily. Ecclesiastes 1:14 says: "I have seen all the works that are done under the sun; and, behold, all is vanity and vexation of spirit." The best condition the world affords to any man contains a great deal of frustration.

Read Ecclesiastes 5:11–16: "When goods increase, they are increased that eat them." If you have much wealth, there will be many mouths to consume it. And what good is there to its owners, save beholding it with their eyes? What good have you really gained? Others consume these goods as well as you. They behold them as well as you. They are not yours; they are the world's goods. You only get to use them for a while. "The sleep of a labouring man is sweet, whether he eat little or much." A poor man who labors hard will enjoy his rest, yet "the abundance of the rich will not suffer him to sleep." Is this not an evil? Further, "there is a sore evil which I have seen under the sun, namely, riches kept for the owners thereof to their hurt." They treasure up riches and keep them to their own demise. How, you may ask, is it to their hurt? Why, they are hurt with the fears and cares that come along with them. The abuse of riches obviously damages their souls. Yet they are also troubled by anxieties about losing their riches, for sometimes fire destroys and thieves take away. Earthly goods are kept to their hurt, and men lie in wait to make a prey of them. But, he says, "Those riches perish by evil travail." People make mistakes that cause them to lose their estate, sometimes by a small word or an act. "And he begetteth a son, and there is nothing in his hand." There is nothing in his hand to do any good or improve what is left to him. "As he came forth of his mother's womb, naked shall he return to go as he came, and shall take nothing of his labour, which he may carry away in his hand." He will not carry away any of the things that he troubled himself to attain. "And this also is a sore evil, that in all points as he came, so shall he go." This is a sore evil, and yet men increase this evil to themselves daily. Surely men will meet with disappointments, trouble, and frustration if they love the things of the world. Therefore, let us avoid loving the world.

It Is Destructive

The love of the world has been the ruin of millions. Hardly any man perishes where his love of the world is not to blame. Philippians 3:19 speaks of those "whose end is destruction, whose God is their belly, and whose glory is in their shame, who mind earthly things." When people mind earthly things, loving the world and its charms, they are headed for doom. They deify their appetites and are always craving more; they must have their pleasures and they always need something else. They praise their own disgrace, reveling in drunkenness, whoredom, and oppression. Honors, pleasure, profit, and power poison the souls of men. "They that will be rich fall into temptation and a snare, and into many foolish and hurtful lusts, which drown men in destruction and perdition" (1 Tim. 6:9). Ill-gotten goods drown men in utter ruin. The Lord Jesus Christ tells us that "it is easier for a camel to go through the eye of a needle, than for a rich man to enter into the kingdom of God" (Matt. 19:24). It is difficult for a man to be both rich and good, to have the abundance of the world and yet be saved.

A man at sea, having made a great voyage and coming near home, found that the ship leaked and was ready to sink. So he filled his pockets with the choicest things he could grab — silver, gold, and jewels. Then, going out of the ship to the smaller boat, he lost his balance due to the weight of the things with which he loaded himself. He dropped into the sea and was seen no more. So many people, through the fullness and weight of their riches, miss the boat that should carry them to heaven and are sunk down into a sea of misery.

Another I have read of, giving away his estate, was asked why he did so. "That I may go the more easily up

Jacob's ladder," he said. Love for the world ruins most men and women. Something or other in it grips their affections and they dote on it to the eternal ruin of their souls. Therefore, we should take heed of that which ruins so many and not allow our hearts to run to it.

It Leaves Us Bitter

If we love the world, God will embitter it to us one way or another. In Jonah 4:6–10, we see how Jonah loved his gourd and was much taken with it. God sent a worm in the night that gnawed the root of it, and the gourd withered away. Then Jonah was perplexed and angry with God for taking away his gourd. Likewise Jacob loved his sons born of Rachel: Joseph and Benjamin. And when they were taken from him, the old man thought that he would go to his grave with sorrow (Gen. 42:38). God embittered to him those things that his heart was set on.

Many men love pleasures, recognition, and honor; sooner or later, for the love of those things, some cross or other will befall them. Many love their children, and God takes them away. Many love their beauty, and God sends some physical illness or adversity that takes it away. Children whom their parents have made idols of prove to be wayward. They turn out to be a matter of sorrow and shame, increasing their parents' fears, cares, and tears. Bitterness is multiplied because they doted on them and loved them inordinately. So it happens when we love the things of this world; if we love them, God will cross us in them. The way to enjoy any mercy is to love it but a little or to love it in order to please God.

Its Pleasures Are Fleeting

We should not love the world because we can neither have nor enjoy its pleasures long. It may be that they will leave us, but if not, we must leave them. And the stronger affections we have toward anything, the more bitter the affliction when we leave it. Strong affections bring great afflictions to men and women. In Luke 12:19–20, we see how short a man's time is. The fool there had built up a great estate: "Thou hast much goods laid up for many years; take thine ease, eat, drink, and be merry. But God said unto him, Thou fool, this night thy soul shall be required of thee: then whose shall those things be, which thou hast provided?" We have many such fools in the world who store up much here, thinking they shall live long and be at ease. As some used to say, "Well, when I have made such a fortune, then I will give up the sea and live at ease." But before that comes, "You fool, this night you are taken away from it in the midst of your pursuit of it." So we cannot long enjoy the things of this world. Therefore, seeing the time is short, as the apostle said, use the world so as not to abuse it. Use the world you may, but do not love it, for then you abuse it. Use the world for your necessities, to further your journey to heaven, to further your accounts before God. But do not abuse it, do not love it. The time is short.

We Were Not Set Apart for It

We should not love the world because we were not set apart for it. Consider that truly godly people are those who are for God and not for the world: "Know that the LORD hath set apart him that is godly for himself" (Ps. 4:3). God has set a godly man apart from the world and set him for Himself. Now if you are set apart for God, will you give yourself to the world? Be for Him who has set you apart for Himself. When a maid is set apart by friends for such a man, she will be for him and not for another; so when God has set you apart from the world, your hearts will be for God and not for the world.

It suggests that a man is a godly man when he is set apart. God calls them out of the world and chooses them for Himself. He will have them to be employed in His way and in His work, and not for the world. A godly man is above the world, and is better than the world. And what? Should he lose himself in the world and mire himself with its charms? Hebrews 11:38 describes the godly as those "of whom the world was not worthy." The world did not think these worthy to live in it, and the world was not worthy of them. Just so precious is a godly man. The soul is a precious thing, more precious than all the world. But when there is precious grace in the soul, it is far beyond the worth of worlds; a thousand worlds are not worth one gracious soul. Therefore do not be for the world, but for God, for whom you are set apart.

It Steals Love from Christ

We should not love the world because such as do love the world do not love the Lord Jesus Christ. As Philippians 3:18 reminds us, "many walk, of whom I have told you often, and now tell you even weeping, that they are the enemies of the cross of Christ." Mark this well, they are neither friends to Christ nor to His cross. They are enemies to the cross of Christ. And who are these enemies? He tells you in verse 19: "who mind earthly things." Men who mind earthly things, the things of this world, are enemies to the cross of Christ.

In James 4:4 the apostle says, "Ye adulterers and adulteresses, know ye not that the friendship of the world is enmity with God? Whosoever therefore will be a friend of the world is the enemy of God." To be an enemy of God and an enemy to Christ is a sad thing. "If any man love not the Lord Jesus Christ, let him be Anathema Maranatha" (1 Cor. 16:22). That is, "Let him be accursed until the Lord comes." One can almost hear Christ saying, "I will come again before long to see who loves Me and who does not. Now if any man does not love Me, let him be accursed until I come and send him to hell, giving him his portion there." Well, then, this should convince us not to love the world; for we cannot love Christ if we love the world. "No man can serve two masters: for either he will hate the one, and love the other; or else he will hold to the one, and despise the other. Ye cannot serve God and mammon" (Matt. 6:24).

It Is Not Our End

We should not love the world because that is neither
the end of our creation nor the end of our redemption;
rather, it crosses the purpose of both. Why was man
created? Man was created for God and for communion
with God. He was made after God's own image — in
knowledge, righteousness, and holiness — so that he
might be a suitable companion (if I may so speak) for
God to converse with and to have familiarity with. Now
if we love the world, what communion do we have with
God? How do we answer the end of our creation? In
Revelation 14:3–4, those gathered around the throne
of the Lamb were "redeemed from the earth" and "from
among men." The end of our creation is to have communion with God, to serve God, and to walk with God.
And the end of our redemption is that we should follow
the Lamb and serve Him in holiness and righteousness
all the days of our lives. Now loving the world stands
opposed to the purpose of creation and redemption. If
we love the world, we will follow the world; if we love
Christ, we will follow Christ. So if you wish not to fight
against the end of your creation and the end of your
redemption, do not love the world or the things of the
world. By this time I trust you are convinced in your
judgments that you should not love the world.

CHAPTER 6

Directions for Getting Our Hearts Off the World

Yes, we should not love the world. However, we find it such a hard thing to follow that we do not know how to pry our affections away from the world and all its charms. What should we do in this case? Consider the following seven directions for getting our hearts off the world.

Be Convinced of Its Evil

If you would have your affections and heart off the world, look well to your ability to make judgments, and do not esteem the world too highly. The reason I say this is because our affections follow the perceptions and judgments made in our minds. If men have strong thoughts about a thing, they will have strong affections. And when men highly esteem things, their hearts are carried out strongly after those things and work vigorously toward them. Now, then, have low thoughts of the world. Judge the world as the Scripture judges it. And how does the Scripture judge the world? Galatians 1:4 describes it as "this present evil world." It is an evil world that is full of sins, full of mischief, full of oppression, full of corruption, subject to bondage, and subject to perishing. It is an evil world full of plots, designs, and devils. Thus the Scripture judges it. Do you judge it so?

In 1 John 5:19 we read that "the whole world lieth in wickedness." You too should judge it so: "Here is a world that lies in wickedness." More literally, it lies in the devil. The devil makes use of the world to deceive you, undo you, and draw you to eternal destruction. Should a man love Sodom, that lay in wickedness? The world is a Sodom that lies in wickedness. Solomon tells you that it is "vanity and vexation of spirit" (Eccl. 1:14). Will you love vanity and vexation of spirit? And 1 John 2:16 says, "All that is in the world, the lust of the flesh, and the lust of the eyes, and the pride of life, is not of the Father, but is of the world." All these strengthen our lusts, and the more our lusts are strengthened, the more grace is hindered and the worse we grow.

But do not let the painted finery of the world deceive and cheat you. What is there in an estate or in power? Men have strange opinions of these things, but see what John says: "The world passeth away, and the lust thereof" (1 John 2:17). It is all a show and scheme; there is no substance in it. What men have low thoughts of, they never dote on. If a woman has low thoughts of a man, she will never love him. The lower thoughts you have, ere long it will be turned to ashes. And will you love ashes? Israel fed on ashes (Isa. 44:20) and Ephraim fed on the wind (Hosea 12:1); they chased vain things, false worship, traditions, inventions of men, and things of this nature. Men and women feed on poor, low things. Well, judge lowly of the world, and do not give a high account of anything in it. It is a world that lies in wickedness, a world that is evil. The more you ponder these things, the more your hearts will be taken off the world.

Mortify Your Lusts

If you do not want to love the world, take pains with your own heart and mortify your lusts. It is our lusts that make us love the world. It is from the wisdom of the flesh that men love the world and the things of the world. Consider Proverbs 23:4: "Labour not to be rich: cease from thine own wisdom." In saying "thine own wisdom," it means the wisdom of your flesh; your corrupt nature makes you desire to be rich. Remember, "the carnal mind is enmity against God" (Rom. 8:7).

Now consider Romans 8:13: "If ye live after the flesh, ye shall die: but if ye through the Spirit do mortify the deeds of the body, ye shall live." Put these lusts to death! Our lusts are deceitful and unruly things; they are craving things that make outrageous claims. Listen to me in this one thing, and if you will but hear me now, I will trouble you no more. But if you do not, they will come again and again, never to be done. Therefore, the best way for us to advance is to mortify our lusts. If we put our lusts to death, we should not love the world. James 4:1–3 says:

> From whence come wars and fightings among you? Come they not hence even of your lusts that war in your members? Ye lust, and have not: ye kill, and desire to have, and cannot obtain: ye fight and war, yet ye have not, because ye ask not. Ye ask, and receive not, because ye ask amiss, that ye may consume it upon your lusts.

Your lusts will beg to have the world — to have honor, power, and riches — yet your soul will not be satisfied. But if our lusts were mortified, all these things would presently be at an end. Sadly, we seek to gratify our lusts, and they undo us.

Look to Things Eternal

If we are to stop loving the world, let us look much at the other world. There is another world. "For unto the angels hath he not put in subjection the world to come" (Heb. 2:5). There is a world to come, and that world is a better world than this world. We read in Hebrews 11:16: "But now they desire a better country, that is, an heavenly." Abraham, Isaac, and the prophets looked at a better country. There is a better world above, with better things than are here in this world. And if we would look at that world — the glory of it, the riches of it, the pleasures of it, the company of it, the latitude of it — we would soon bid this world farewell. That world makes this one look like a dream, a shadow, a picture, as nothing. We are encouraged in 2 Corinthians 4:18 to "look not at the things which are seen, but at the things which are not seen: for the things which are seen are temporal; but the things which are not seen are eternal." There are things not seen in this world. These things are eternal things. They are eternal riches, the eternal God, the Lord Jesus, glorious angels, the saints, and rivers of pleasure at the right hand of God. Look at these things, and your hearts will be taken off of this world.

Diligently Guard Your Heart

If we are to get our hearts off the world, which is a very necessary thing, then we must guard our hearts with all diligence. Look as attentively to your heart as to your eyes, to the meat you eat, to your life. Keep it with all diligence. Look to your affections and do not let them rove and wander up and down in the world, ranging here and there. Look to your fears, for many are afraid of poverty — afraid they will have to live and pay every man his own, while not being able to support themselves. But in Matthew 6:25–26 Christ says this:

> Take no thought for your life, what ye shall eat, or what ye shall drink; nor yet for your body, what ye shall put on. Is not the life more than meat, and the body than raiment? Behold the fowls of the air: for they sow not, neither do they reap,

nor gather into barns; yet your heavenly Father
feedeth them. Are ye not much better than they?

That is, "You poor creatures, do not fear poverty, or that
you will not have meat, drink, and clothes. The birds are
never afraid and they have nobody to look after them.
You feed your tame birds indeed, but who provides for
the wild ones? God provides for them." Look well to your
fears, for they often drive people to love the world.

Look well to your love, so that you take complacency in no creature whatsoever. Rather, love the Lord,
taking complacency in God and Christ. You know that
Christ said that "thou shalt love the Lord thy God with
all thy heart, and with all thy soul, and with all thy
strength, and with all thy mind" (Luke 10:27). Now, if
God has our all, what will the creature have? But the
creatures have our love, and God has little or nothing.
Here is our great failing, yet here is "all" used four times.
God should have all of our heart, soul, strength, and
mind, leaving creatures to have little or none.

Look well to your desires. Men are creatures of
desire, crying, "oh, that I had this or that." But God
said, "Thou shalt not covet" (Ex. 20:17). That is, "Be
content with such things as ye have" (Heb.13:5). We
should not covet anything of the world. Instead, we
should follow our callings and leave events to God. If
God casts something before us, take it thankfully and
use it well to His glory.

Submit to God's Will

If you desire to stop loving the world, submit your will to God's will. God is infinitely wise and infinitely good. He is the great Sovereign, and His will is not to be disputed. God's will must take place. Now what is the will of God? Here is His will: "Labour not to be rich: cease from thine own wisdom" (Prov. 23:4). Now if our wills were subordinate to His will, there would be no loving the world. Whether I have little or much of the world, it is all the same to me, for I seek the will of God. Whether God gives me something or nothing, I will be content.

Look on Christ

If you would have your heart removed from the things of the world, behold the crucified and glorified Lord Jesus Christ. Set Christ crucified often before your eyes, and look on Him with the eye of faith. "God forbid that I should glory, save in the cross of our Lord Jesus Christ, by whom the world is crucified unto me, and I unto the world" (Gal. 6:14). That is, "I look on Christ crucified, and by the eye of faith I can see Him hanging there, and all the glory of the world stained there. Is all the world comparable to Christ? There is the King, the High Priest, the Mediator, the great Prophet. There is the Heir of the world crucified. There is His blood running down. He has laid down His life for sinners, and to take my heart off from the world." If you look on a dead man, it deadens your spirit. What will looking on Christ do then? It will deaden your heart toward the world if you look on Jesus Christ crucified. "I am crucified to the world," said Paul.

Then look on Christ glorified, and your heart will be raised above the world. "If ye then be risen with Christ, seek those things which are above, where Christ sitteth on the right hand of God. Set your affection on things above, not on things on the earth" (Col. 3:1–2). Christ has died, risen, and gone to glory. If now you are risen out of the state of sin, transferred from the power of darkness into the kingdom of God's dear Son, you will have your heart where Christ is. Consider Christ in this way: "There is my Head, my King, my Husband. There is my Redeemer, the one who is a thousand times better than the world. Therefore, I will not set my heart on things of the earth, but on things above. How glorious it is to see the King in His glory!" Look much, and consider much of Christ crucified and glorified.

Love God More

If we would keep our hearts from loving the world, we must love God Himself more. The more our love for God grows, the more our hearts will be estranged from the world. In loving God more, we will view creation for what it is, and God as infinitely more valuable than the world and all that is in it. The world is an evil thing, full of corruption. Scripture speaks of "having escaped the corruption that is in the world through lust" (2 Peter 1:4). Lusts corrupt the world, leaving it full of loathsomeness. But look on the beauties of God, for the excellencies of God are such as would ravish a man's soul and draw it up to Him.

Conclusion

And so, in closing this book, consider again our text: "Love not the world, neither the things that are in the world. If any man love the world, the love of the Father is not in him" (1 John 2:15). Take it this way: if your heart is wedded to the world, the Father does not love you. Or you may take it another way: you do not love the Father if your affections are chained to the world. Therefore, if you want evidence that the Father loves you and that you love the Father, stop loving the world. Instead, let your love abound more and more for the Father. Then you will have more and more evidence of His love, and evidence that you do not love the world. Thus you see many arguments, remedies, and helps for getting our hearts off the world. May the Lord make them effectual.

Some other
Puritan Resources

from
**REFORMATION
HERITAGE BOOKS**

Sound-Hearted Christian

William Greenhill

Introduced by Joel R. Beeke

978-1-60178-099-7   Hardback, 240 pages

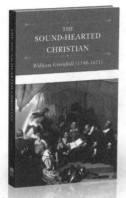

Nearing the end of his life and ministry, William Greenhill left his congregation a parting gift and lasting testimony of his pastoral care for their souls — he published *The Sound-Hearted Christian*. This book developed from a series of sermons Greenhill preached on Psalm 119:80, "Let my heart be sound in thy statutes; that I be not ashamed." Greenhill shows that a sound heart is watchful and attentive, recognizing that our soul is our greatest possession. After demonstrating the excellence and desirability of a sound heart, he challenges us to test the soundness of our heart. He then directs and motivates us to get and keep a sound heart. The book ends with several appended sermons on faith, Christ, and God's Word, which serve as further encouragements to establishing and maintaining a sound heart.

"In William Greenhill, a renowned preacher and eminent scholar, you have a trustworthy guide into this vitally important subject—what it means to be a sound-hearted Christian."

— J. Stephen Yuille, Pastor at
Grace Community Church in Glen Rose,
Texas, and author of *Puritan Spirituality*

Meet the Puritans

Joel R. Beeke and Randall J. Pederson

978-1-60178-000-3   Hardback, 935 pages

Meet the Puritans provides a biographical and theological introduction to the Puritans whose works have been reprinted in the last fifty years, and also gives helpful summaries and insightful analyses of those reprinted works. It contains nearly 150 biographical entries, and nearly 700 summaries of reprinted works. A very useful resource for getting into the Puritans.

> "As furnaces burn with ancient coal and not with the leaves that fall from today's trees, so my heart is kindled with the fiery substance I find in the old Scripture-steeped sermons of Puritan pastors. A warm thanks to the authors of *Meet the Puritans* for all the labor to make them known."
>
> —John Piper, Pastor,
> Bethlehem Baptist Church,
> Minneapolis, Minnesota

The Fading of the Flesh and The Flourishing of Faith

George Swinnock
Edited by J. Stephen Yuille

978-1-60178-072-0   Paperback, 184 pages

The Puritans frequently talked about dying well. That is something we do not discuss much these days, though we should. Expounding Psalm 73:26, "My flesh and my heart faileth: but God is the strength of my heart, and my portion for ever," Swinnock combines careful explanation with vivid illustration to reveal the futility of earthly comforts and highlight the inestimable comfort, satisfaction, and joy afforded us in Christ.

"This wonderful little book, written with charm, simplicity, and clarity by George Swinnock is bound to prove both a delight and a challenge to any Christian who values the riches of the gospel. It is a spiritual gem that deserves to be read and re-read. In addition, its charm, simplicity, and clarity make it a perfect entry point to the writings of the pastoral Puritans. Beautifully edited for the modern reader by Dr. Stephen Yuille, *The Fading of the Flesh* is a rare spiritual treat."

— Sinclair B. Ferguson, Senior Minister
of the First Presbyterian Church
in Columbia, South Carolina

John Owen

Simonetta Carr

Illustrated by Matt Abraxas

978-1-60178-088-1

Hardback, 64 pages
For Ages 7–12

John Owen was a great Puritan preacher who lived in England. In this book, Simonetta Carr informs readers about Owen's life, revealing some of the things that interested him while in school, the care he showed to people when he became a pastor, and the influential books that he wrote. Readers will also come to understand the difficult times in which Owen lived, and how he handled the terrors of war and religious persecution. Full of illustrations and fascinating information, this is an ideal way for young readers to learn history.

"In clear, unembellished language Simonetta Carr chronicles the life of the 'Prince of Puritans' through a tumultuous period of English history. This book manages to be simple without being shallow. Young readers will admire the integrity of Owen's conscience as a man living in a difficult time and relish the rich descriptions of Owen's theological genius. This is a masterful book. I trust that many others will follow."

—Tedd Tripp, Pastor of Grace
Fellowship Church and author
of *Shepherding a Child's Heart*

"A Habitual Sight of Him":
The Christ-centered Piety of
Thomas Goodwin

Introduced and edited by Joel R. Beeke and Mark Jones

978-1-60178-067-6   Paperback, 152 pages

Thomas Goodwin (1600–1680) was a faithful pastor, Westminster divine, advisor to Oliver Cromwell, and president of Magdalen College, Oxford. In this book, Joel R. Beeke and Mark Jones acquaint the reader with Goodwin through an informative biographical introduction. The remainder of the book, 35 selections from the writings of Goodwin, displays Goodwin's constant attention to Christ in his various theological convictions. You will learn much about the life and teaching of this influential Puritan, and perhaps, be strengthened with a habitual sight of Christ.

> "Christology lay at the very heart of the best of Reformed Orthodox theology and practice. In this short book the reader is not only introduced to a brilliant Puritan theologian but also to the very center of his vital Christian piety. I hope this book introduces the writings of Goodwin to a new generation."
>
> — Carl Trueman, Professor of Historical Theology and Church History, Westminster Theological Seminary, Philadelphia

The Market Day of the Soul

James T. Dennison, Jr.

978-1-60178-037-9   Paperback, 222 pages

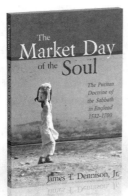

In *The Market Day of the Soul*, James T. Dennison, Jr. examines the question of the supreme Christian holy day, the Sabbath. He shows how the Sabbath emerged from the imprecision of the sixteenth century to become a celebrated cause in pre-Revolutionary England. Finally, he demonstrates triumph of the Puritan Sabbath during the Revolution, a triumph that continued to make the English Sabbath distinctive into the nineteenth century. In the course of this investigation, Dennison shows that the Puritan view of the Lord's Day became the dominant view—both theologically and practically—by the latter half of the seventeenth century.

"Dennison's detailed, historical study of the Sabbath—particularly the Puritan Sabbath—provides numerous insights that will help Christians today to maintain God-honoring Sabbath-keeping as the market day of the soul. May God use this book to turn many from the soul-damaging results of neglecting to keep the Sabbath day to the conscientious keeping of Sabbath as a delight owed to God (Isa. 58:13–14)."

—Joel R. Beeke, President
of Puritan Reformed Theological
Seminary, Grand Rapids